THE VALUE OF HELPING

The Story of Harriet Tubman

VALUE COMMUNICATIONS, INC.
PUBLISHERS
LA JOLLA, CALIFORNIA

THE VALUE OF HELPING

The Story of
Harriet Tubman

BY ANN DONEGAN JOHNSON

First Edition
Manufactured in the United States of America
For information write to: ValueTales, P.O. Box 1012
La Jolla, CA 92038

Library of Congress Cataloging in Publication Data

Johnson, Ann Donegan.
      The value of helping.

      (ValueTales)
      SUMMARY: Describes the helpful work of Harriet
Tubman in aiding slaves to flee the South, in assisting the
Union army during the Civil War, and in establishing homes
for the old and needy after the war.
      1.   Tubman, Harriet Ross, 1815?-1913—Juvenile
literature.   2.   Underground railroad—Juvenile literature.
3.   Slavery in the United States—Fugitive slaves—Juvenile
literature.   4.   Slaves—United States—Biography—
Juvenile literature.   5.   Afro-Americans—Biography—
Juvenile literature.   6.   Altruism—Juvenile
[1.   Tubman, Harriet Ross, 1815?-1913   2.   Afro-
Americans—Biography.   3.   Helpfulness]   I.   Title.
E444.T82J63   301.44′93′0924   [B]   [92]   79-21652

ISBN 0-916392-41-4

Dedicated to Richard Lewak whose help I have dearly appreciated.

This tale is about a person who helped many people, Harriet Tubman. The story that follows is based on events in her life. More historical facts about Harriet Tubman can be found on page 63.

Once upon a time...

a little girl named Harriet lived in a cabin in the fields near Bucktown, Maryland. She slept in a corner on a mattress stuffed with straw. Sometimes when she woke up in the morning she felt tired and stiff, and her bones ached.

But no matter how she felt, Harriet was out of bed at dawn. She had to hurry to light the fires in the big house. Then she had to sweep and dust. And even though she was only seven years old herself, she had to help look after the baby.

Harriet wasn't an ordinary little girl, you see. She was a black slave.

Many years before, Harriet's grandparents had been kidnapped from their village in Africa. They had been brought to America and sold as slaves. And so their children and grandchildren, who were born in America, were slaves, too. They had no rights at all.

If he wanted to, Harriet's master could make her work from dawn until midnight in the big house. Or he could send her out to help the slaves who worked in the fields. At harvest time Harriet and the other slaves picked corn all day long and late into the night.

Harriet's master could even hire his slaves out. Because Harriet was small, she was often sent out to do housework. Sometimes the mistress of a house was kind to the child, but just as often Harriet was treated like a little animal.

"Useless, stupid girl!" cried one woman. She had a whip and she used the whip on Harriet.

Harriet cringed away. "But I tried to sweep the floor real clean!" she sobbed.

"Now you're being insolent!" shouted the woman. "Don't you dare talk back to me!" And she struck Harriet again.

But life wasn't all work for Harriet and the older slaves in Bucktown. There were quiet evenings, and there was one old man who had learned to read. He had a Bible, and he liked to read Bible stories to the children.

Harriet's favorite story was the one about the children of Israel who were captives in Egypt.

"They were slaves just like us," said Harriet. "Old Pharaoh treated them just like the white folks treat us. I wonder if we'll ever get anyone to help us, the way Moses helped the children of Israel to get out of Egypt?"

"Maybe we will, child," said the old man, "but you'd better not let the master hear you talking that way, or he'll beat you till he plumb wears his arm out!"

So Harriet didn't talk. But she could sing, and she began to sing quietly. It was a song that many of her people knew:

Go down, Moses,
Way down in Egypt's land.
Tell ole Pharaoh,
Let my people go.

Singing wasn't all the slaves did when their long day's work was done. At night in the cabins they whispered about places where black people could be free.

"There aren't any slaves in the North," said one man. "All the people there are free men and women."

"Even in the South, lots of white folks don't believe in slavery," said another. "Those folks are helping blacks escape to the North."

"Just like Moses," said Harriet to herself. She felt a wonderful excitement. She kept still about it for a long time. But one evening, when she and her father were walking beside the river, she began to talk about freedom.

"Shush, child!" said her father. "You're too young to be thinking that way. It's dangerous to try to escape."

"But Daddy Ben," said Harriet, "don't I have a right to be free?"

"Yes you do, child," old Ben answered, "but later, Harriet. When you're grown. Then you'll go north."

Ben pointed. "You see that star up there?" he said. "The big one that never moves? That's the North Star. When you go, you keep that star in front of you. It will take you to freedom!"

After that Harriet watched the stars every night, and she dreamed of the time when she could run away to freedom. The wonderful North Star never moved, of course. But one night, when Harriet was dreaming her exciting dreams, she saw another star drop from the sky.

"A shooting star!" said Harriet.

Then she blinked. The shooting star wasn't acting like any shooting star Harriet had ever seen. It fell straight toward her, and it got bigger and bigger as it came. At last it landed right at her feet.

"I'm dreaming," said Harriet to herself.

Then she was sure she heard the star say, "Harriet, I've come to help you find your way to freedom. And there are lots of other people who want to help you, too."

"This is silly," thought Harriet. "Stars don't talk. But I like what this one is saying. I think I'll go right on listening to it."

"If people help you," said the star, "then you can turn around and help other slaves escape."

"That surely makes sense," said Harriet. She decided that she would keep the star with her, and she'd name it Twinkle. "It's a good name for a star," she said, "and it will be fun to have someone who can share my dreams."

Harriet waited patiently after that, and she grew, although she never grew very big. Then, one day when she was working in the fields, she saw another slave put down his hoe.

"I'm just going to step up to the village," he said. "I want to get something at the store." Then he walked away.

"Oh, Twinkle!" whispered Harriet. "I'm afraid. That man has tried to escape so many times, and he always gets caught. Look. The overseer is going after him now."

"Then perhaps we'd better go after him, too," said Twinkle.

Twinkle and Harriet hurried to the village store. When they got there, they saw that the overseer was terribly angry.

"That man's trying to run away again!" shouted the overseer. He motioned to some black men who were watching. "Tie him up!" he ordered. "And you, girl. You help them. I'm going to give that man a beating he'll never forget!"

But the men didn't move. Harriet didn't move. And the slave decided to run for his life!

The overseer started to run after the slave. But suddenly there was a little black girl standing in the doorway.

"Out of my way, girl!" the overseer shouted.

Harriet didn't move.

"All right!" said the overseer, and he picked up a big metal weight and threw it.

"Watch out!" cried Twinkle.

It was too late. The weight caught Harriet on the side of the head.

18

For months after that, Harriet lay in a corner of the cabin where she lived with her mother and father. She was very weak and very ill, and it seemed that surely she would die.

"Freedom!" she whispered to herself. "I want freedom!"

"Get well and strong and you'll have freedom," promised Twinkle.

Slowly Harriet did get well, and when she finally could move around again, she found that she had gained an inner strength. "I hate slavery," she said, "and I'm going to do something about it!"

Harriet needed all her inner strength, for she never completely got over the blow on her head. She had strange times when she would be going about her work and suddenly she would fall asleep.

"She's a dimwit!" said the overseer.

But Harriet was far from a dimwit. She watched and she listened, and when the slaves began talking among themselves about a thing called the Underground Railroad, she heard them.

"Just what is this Underground Railroad?" asked Twinkle.

"Well, it doesn't have a thing to do with steam engines," said Harriet. "It's just a way that white people and black people help slaves escape to the free states in the North. They lead them along roads that are safe. Sometimes they go by water. And when they have to stop and rest, they hide in houses that are safe—places that they call 'stations' on the railroad."

"That's wonderful!" said Twinkle. "And it's people helping people, just the way Moses helped the children of Israel."

"Someday I'm going to take that Underground Railroad," Harriet declared. "I'm going to get away to the North."

But before Harriet could do this, she fell in love with a free Negro named John Tubman. "He's so nice, Twinkle," she said. "He's happy and carefree. I like being with him."

"I suppose you're going to marry him," said Twinkle.

"Indeed I am," said Harriet.

She did marry John Tubman when she was twenty-four. But it wasn't long before she began to grow impatient with her husband. True, he could spend his wages as he pleased, and he didn't have to call any man master. But there were many things he couldn't do. He couldn't own land. He couldn't vote. He couldn't even move about as he pleased. What's more, he didn't seem to care that he wasn't really free.

"I'm perfectly happy the way I am," he said when he heard Harriet talk about the free states in the North. "I don't want to run away—and I don't want to hear any talk about you running away, either!"

So Harriet stopped talking to her husband about her dreams, but she never stopped dreaming.

"If you ever get away, you'll have to go without John," warned Twinkle. "Can you do that?"

Harriet nodded. "Freedom means more to me even than John does," she said. "But maybe I won't have to run away. Maybe I can save enough money to buy myself free."

Harriet was trying to do this—selling pies from door to door in Bucktown—when she met a lady who was a Quaker.

The Quakers were very much against slavery, and there was something about Harriet that interested this Quaker lady. "Do you want to be free?" she asked Harriet. "If you do, I can send you to people who'll help you on your way."

"Do I want to be free?" Harriet echoed. "I've been waiting for this chance for years!"

Harriet went home then, walking very fast. She didn't say a word to her husband, for she knew that he would never come with her. But she did tell her brothers Robert and William what the Quaker lady had told her.

25

"We're to follow the Choptank River to the border of Maryland and Delaware," she said. "Then we should take the road to Camden. In Camden we'll get help."

"It will be dangerous, but we'll chance it," said Robert.

"If we don't go now, we'll never be free," William decided.

They all set out, walking through the dark woods at night. "Don't be afraid," said Harriet. "Daddy Ben always said if we followed the North Star it would take us to freedom."

They had not gone far, however, before William decided that the woods were too dark, even with the North Star. And Robert was sure they would never make it. The two young men turned back toward Bucktown.

"Don't give up, Harriet," whispered Twinkle. "You can do it. Even if you *are* only five feet tall, you're as strong as any man, and you've got courage to spare."

Harriet needed her courage. She went on for fifteen nights, struggling through the darkness. She tumbled into holes, and she tore her clothes on the briars. In the daytime she hid in barns and cellars, for there were men out everywhere searching for runaway slaves.

When she reached Camden, there were people to help her. They passed her along from one to another until at last she crossed the state line into Pennsylvania.

"Oh, Twinkle, I feel as if I'm in heaven!" she said, after she got to Philadelphia. "I'm going to help my family get to freedom, just the way all the wonderful people on the Underground Railroad helped me!"

"You can help more if you have money," said Twinkle.

"Of course!" said Harriet, and she went to work. She washed clothes and scrubbed floors. She cooked and she sewed. And she could hardly believe what was happening when people gave her money for her labors.

"Back at Bucktown I did the same things, and I never got a dime," she said to Twinkle.

But even after she had some money, Harriet wasn't sure she was ready to go back for her family. "It's so dangerous," she said. "I'm afraid I'll just get them into trouble."

Then she heard of a man named William Still. He was a black man who was fighting slavery, and he knew everything there was to know about the Underground Railroad. He even kept records on all the escaped slaves who came through Philadelphia. Then, if their relatives came after them, he could tell them where they had gone.

"I'll talk to William Still," Harriet decided. "He can help me if anyone can."

"Please, Mr. Still," Harriet said, when she met this famous man. "I want to get my family out of the South. I want to be a conductor on the Underground Railroad."

William Still just smiled at first. Conductors on the Underground Railroad weren't at all like the conductors on regular railways—the ones who cried, "All aboard!" and punched people's tickets. Conductors on the Underground Railroad had to lead groups of runaway slaves to safety. They had to find their way through dark woods and treacherous swamps. It was rugged work, and very dangerous.

"Harriet, conductors on the railroad are always men," said William Still.

"I've done men's work all my life," said Harriet. "And I'm determined. I've even bought myself a man's suit."

William Still smiled. "All right. I think perhaps you can do it," he said.

And indeed Harriet could. On her first trip south, she brought out her sister and two of her sister's children. There were many other slaves with them, and Harriet led them all to freedom just as Moses led the children of Israel out of Egypt.

After Harriet's first journey with her sister, she made many trips back to the South. Sometimes she brought out members of her family. Sometimes the black people she brought out weren't related to her at all.

Soon she was one of the better-known conductors on the Underground Railroad.

''The slave-hunters don't like you even a little bit,'' laughed Twinkle. ''They'd dearly love to get their hands on you.''

''I'm not going to give them a chance,'' declared Harriet.

But then a very sad thing happened. A law was passed that, if a runaway slave was caught in the North, he could be returned to his master in the South.

''How terrible!'' moaned Twinkle. ''Now the slave-hunters will be everywhere!''

''I won't let that stop me,'' said Harriet. ''I'll go right on helping my people. But now I'll take them all the way to Canada. They'll be safe there!''

But then word came to Harriet that her father was in trouble. He was still in Bucktown, and he had been caught helping a slave to escape.

"It's time your parents made that trip to Canada," Twinkle told Harriet.

"It's past time," said Harriet, and she went to Bucktown. Her parents were both past eighty and unable to walk the long distances over rough roads and through the woods to safety. From junk Harriet made a cart of sorts. She fastened a couple of boards to an axle that had two wheels. Then she hitched an ancient horse with a straw collar to the axle. She had a chariot to carry her mother and father to freedom.

Soon Harriet had led so many slaves to freedom that people began to call her Moses.

"Remember the song you used to sing?" said Twinkle. "It was about Moses talking to old Pharaoh."

"I remember," said Harriet, "but there weren't any reward posters in Egypt. Right now there are posters up everywhere offering big rewards for my capture. Just think of it, Twinkle! One of the posters says I'm worth $40,000!"

There weren't only the reward posters for Harriet. There were meetings and conventions all through Maryland, and the slave owners talked and argued and worried and wondered about her.

"We've got to stop the runaways," said one man. "We've got to get the woman called Moses!"

"Slaves disappear from my plantation every week!" another complained.

"If we don't watch out, we'll soon have no one to work our fields or look after our houses," said a third.

Harriet would have chuckled with glee if she could have heard this. Of course she couldn't hear it, so she just went on helping her people every chance she got.

In 1861 war broke out between the North and the South.

"Twinkle, I must do something to help," said Harriet. "If the North wins, perhaps slavery will be ended in America."

By now Harriet knew many important people. She talked to them, trying to find a way to serve her country. Everyone was kind to her, but everyone told her the same thing. "Negroes aren't allowed in the army," they said. "You'll just have to be patient and wait."

Harriet tried patience and she tried waiting, and at last Governor
Andrews of Massachusetts sent for her. He was her friend, and he
admired the work she had done.

"Harriet, many of your people are escaping from their masters
and joining the Union forces in South Carolina," he said. "Some
of them are sick. They need to be cared for. Do you want to go to them?"

"You know that I do, Governor," replied Harriet.

41

Again Harriet headed south. This time she went all the way to South Carolina, to the Union army base where there was a hospital for Negroes. She went to work in the wards, and although there was very little in the way of medicine and supplies, she did everything she could to help the men there.

Of course many of Harriet's patients had already heard of this wonderful woman called Moses. Some of them were runaways, just as she had been. Some of them wanted to help, just as she did. They had come to be cooks and handymen at the base, because they weren't allowed to be soldiers.

But while Harriet was in South Carolina, a wonderful thing happened.

For the first time black men were admitted to the army. The first regiment of Negro soldiers, the Fifty-fourth Regiment, was formed in Massachusetts, and the men were sent to South Carolina.

"Look, Twinkle!" cried Harriet, when the men arrived. "My people are fighting for their freedom!"

44

"Yes, and don't they look proud in their uniforms," said Twinkle.

"I'm proud, too," said Harriet. "I'm going to see what I can do for them, Twinkle."

And from that time on she cooked and washed and ran errands for the black soldiers of the Fifty-fourth.

Colonel Robert Gould Shaw commanded the regiment, and he was a white man. It wasn't long before he learned about Harriet and her work for the Underground Railroad. He sent word to her and asked her to come to see him.

"I need people who are familiar with the territory around here," he told her. "You must know this area very well."

"Indeed I do," said Harriet.

"Do you think you could organize a group to scout for us?" asked the colonel. "We need to know what the Confederate forces are doing."

"I'd be proud to help," responded Harriet. And even though Twinkle whispered that it might be dangerous, Harriet organized a group of southern Negroes to do this work.

"Some of you know the hills and the swamps around here," she told her men. "Some of you have worked on the roads or the railroads. I want you to go out and scout the countryside. Then come back and tell me about the movements of the Confederate soldiers."

Harriet's men were very loyal, and they brought back every bit of information they could gather. Harriet passed the reports along, and because of her scouts, the Union forces led many successful raids in the area.

Harriet didn't leave all of the dangerous work to others. Sometimes she went on scouting trips herself.

On one trip she scouted along the bank of the Combahee River with her men. They counted the explosive devices that had been anchored in the river, and they noted exactly where these torpedoes were.

Harriet noted something else. "There are so many plantations on either side of the river, Twinkle," she said. "Just think of the slaves on those plantations. Surely lots of them want to escape."

"I think you're planning something special," said Twinkle.

"Wait and see," said Harriet. Then she hurried back to the army base and asked to see Colonel James Montgomery. He was an expert on guerrilla warfare.

"I've just come from the Combahee River," Harriet told him. "There are plantations along both sides of that river, and there must be hundreds of slaves there. Surely some of them would join the Union forces if we could free them."

The colonel nodded. "Well and good," he said, "but we'd better plan carefully. We don't want to lose more men than we gain."

Harriet and Montgomery plotted their attack carefully. They took three gunboats and three hundred Negro troops, and they sailed up the Combahee. They went slowly so that Harriet could point out the torpedoes. As they went, the Union soldiers lifted the explosives out of the water. Then they set fire to the plantations.

"We're driving the slaveholders back!" one man shouted to Harriet.

"Good!" she cried. "Now get all the slaves on board!"

When they returned to the base, they had completed one of the most successful raids of the entire war. They had freed more than 750 slaves.

Harriet was happy for her people, who were now safe in the army base. She was more than a bit happy for herself, too. She was the first and only woman in American history to have planned and led a military campaign.

As the war came to an end, Harriet decided to go to her home in Auburn, New York. Her parents were there now, and she wanted to see them.

She had a pass that entitled her to travel for half fare because she was an army nurse. She took the pass and boarded the train in South Carolina.

52

Harriet had scarcely settled herself for the trip when the conductor came through the car. He wouldn't even look at Harriet's pass.

"You're lying!" he said. "You don't have any right to travel for half fare. You don't even have any right to be on this train! No woman can travel as a soldier—especially if she's a Negro woman."

Then, because Harriet wouldn't get off the train, the conductor got three strong men to help him. They seized poor Harriet and shoved her into the baggage compartment, and she made her journey north lying on the floor, bruised and wretched.

"Twinkle, we have a long way to go before we're really free," she said sadly.

Twinkle couldn't answer, for Harriet was right.

Of course Harriet wasn't quiet about the terrible thing that had happened to her. "I'm going to tell the newspapers," she said. "Then perhaps I can help my people still more. Our struggle for freedom isn't over, and it will never be over while we're treated so badly just because we're black."

When the story of Harriet's encounter with the conductor was published, people were indignant.

"How could he do that?" they said. "Harriet Tubman has risked her life many times to help other people. How could he treat her that way?"

"How could he treat *anyone* that way?" said other people. "We have to work to make sure it doesn't happen any more."

"Real freedom for black people will be slow in coming," said Harriet. "They'll need help for a long time to come."

Harriet went to her little house in Auburn, and she did everything she could for Negroes who were in distress.

"Of course it would be easier if I had some money," she told Twinkle. "If only the government would pay me for the work I did during the war."

But the government didn't pay Harriet. For many years she had to rely on her wealthy friends for the money she needed to help the poor ones. Then, when Harriet was an old lady of eighty, a wonderful thing happened.

"Twinkle, I've had word from Washington," she said. "They've given me twenty dollars—and they're going to give me twenty dollars every single month for the rest of my life! It's a pension for my war work!"

Twinkle laughed. "I have a feeling you won't keep much of that money for yourself," he said. "I have a feeling you'll use it the way you use everything—to help other people."

57

Twinkle was absolutely right. Harriet did use her money to help people. Although she was eighty herself, she felt sorry for old folks who had no place to go, so she founded a home for them in Auburn. Another home was established in her name in Boston.

"I'm getting to be almost as famous now as when I was a conductor on the Underground Railroad," thought Harriet. "And I'm not through yet."

Then she bought twenty-five acres of land near her home. "That will be my free farm," she said. "It's going to be a place that will be run by Negro people for Negro people."

In March 1913, Harriet was more than ninety years old. She was very frail and very ill, but she was never lonely. People who help other people don't have time to be lonely.

"I think my end is coming, Twinkle," she said. "I want to have my friends with me. I want to say good-bye to them."

Harriet had many friends and they all came. Harriet herself led them in a farewell service, and together they sang their good-bye to her. It wasn't a sad good-bye, either. They sang:

> *I got a robe.*
> *You got a robe.*
> *All God's children's got a robe.*
> *When I get to heaven, going to put on my robe.*
> *Going to shout all over God's heaven!"*

It has been more than seventy years since Harriet Tubman said good-bye to her friends, and more than a hundred years since she risked her life as a conductor on the Underground Railroad. Many things have changed. But today there are still people who need help, and there are people who enjoy helping.

You're the only one who can decide about the value of helping in your life. Do you know people who would be happier if you helped them? And would that make you happier, too? Would you feel good about yourself?

Just like our little friend Harriet Tubman.

The End

Historical Facts ·

Harriet Tubman, a slave, was born about 1820 in a small village called Bucktown in Dorchester County, Maryland. Her grandparents on both sides were blacks who had been brought to America from Africa sometime after 1725.

Very early in her life, Harriet witnessed the inhumanities of slavery. She personally endured hard labor and many beatings, and she developed a rebellious nature. She was determined to be free, but she was careful to hide this fact from her white masters.

When she was fifteen, Harriet saw another slave trying to escape. She deliberately got in the way of the overseer, who was giving chase. In a rage, the man struck her in the head with a two-pound iron counterweight. For months after this savage attack, Harriet was near death.

Harriet never completely recovered from this incident. It left her with a dent in her skull, and with strange seizures during which she would suddenly fall asleep. But her desire to be free was fiercer than ever.

In 1844, Harriet married a free Negro named John Tubman. He was a man completely satisfied with his lot, and he had no patience when Harriet talked of freedom.

In 1849, Harriet decided that she could endure slavery no longer. She set out at night, accompanied by two of her brothers, and bound for the Delaware border. The brothers soon lost heart and turned back, but Harriet succeeded in making her way to Delaware and then to Pennsylvania.

Harriet worked in Philadelphia, earning money so that she could try to get her parents out of the South. She soon became involved with the Underground Railroad, an elaborate network of routes and guides and hiding places that helped runaway slaves reach safety in the northern states. As early as 1850 there was a record of her acting as a guide or "conductor" for the railroad.

Harriet soon became one of the most active conductors, earning for herself the name Moses. In spite of the fact that there were wanted posters with her description in most towns and that at one time the reward offered for her capture amounted to $40,000, she went on with her work.

HARRIET TUBMAN
ca. 1821–1913

She helped at least three hundred slaves escape. Many of these were members of her own family.

After the Fugitive Slave Law was passed in 1850, Harriet's work became more difficult. She had to guide escaped slaves all the way to Canada, because the northern states were no longer safe.

In the years immediately before the Civil War, Harriet became good friends with many prominent Abolitionists. When the war came, she volunteered her services, and she worked as a nurse, laundress, cook, and spy for the Union army in South Carolina.

After the war she returned to a small house she had bought in Auburn, New York. There she cared for her elderly parents and also housed and fed many black people who were in need. Throughout her long life, she continued to work for full freedom for Negroes.

She was still active when she was eighty, and she appeared on platforms with leaders such as Susan B. Anthony and Elizabeth Cady Stanton. She finally did receive a pension from the government for her work during the Civil War, and this money helped fund her homes for the needy.

Harriet was ninety-three when she contracted pneumonia. She died on March 10, 1913. A bronze plaque on the Cayuga County Courthouse in Auburn is a tribute to this great American woman.

The ValueTale Series